This book, *ALL ABOUT TREES (IN & AROUND HOUSTON)* will tell you all that you need to know to maintain your trees **if you live in or around Houston**. There are more than 20,000 different kinds of trees in the world, 1,000 in the United States alone. But in Houston, there are only a dozen or so trees that I plan to discuss. Chances are these are the ones you have. So this book is specializing, especially for you.

I'll tell you which trees grow the fastest, the ones that live the longest, and how to plant them. I'll tell you trees that are **best** for Houston according to climate and soil conditions and how to care for them, trim them, and treat them for any ailment they might have and, most important, when to call on an expert.

My father was in the tree business since 1968. As a young boy, I tagged along with him whenever I could. He taught me *ALL ABOUT TREES.* My staff and I have continued to learn by keeping current with the improved methods of caring for trees. Everything we know that is pertinent for you to know about your trees, this book will tell you. Whatever you can't understand or want explained in greater detail, just call me by dialing:

F-O-S-T-E-R-S

John Foster

ALL ABOUT TREES

IN & AROUND HOUSTON

by

John Foster

Swan Publishing
New York ❖ California ❖ Texas

Author: John Foster
Editors: Pete Billac & Mel Diamond
Cover Design: Cindy Coker
Layout Design: Sharon Davis
Photo of John Foster by: Wayne Lieber
Silverpoint Drawing of Ove Foster by: Robert Annesley
Technical Consultants: Kenny Grayson & Eric Grayson
Proof Readers: Selena Foster & Mark Early
Illustrations by: Melisa (Lisa) Foster

ALL ABOUT TREES IN & AROUND HOUSTON is available in quantity discounts through SWAN Publishing, 126 Live Oak, Alvin, TX 77511. (281) 388-2547 or FAX (281) 585-3738.

Printed in the United States of America.

This book is dedicated to the memory of my father, Ove Foster, who not only began Foster's Tree Service in 1968 to care for the trees in and around Houston, but who also gave me my love and concern for trees.

INTRODUCTION

As is the case with all the books I edit and publish, I give the introduction. I do it because I get to know the author, having spent hours and hours with them while working on the book, and I can introduce the author better than they can—what I mean is, I can say *nice* things about them without it sounding too self-serving.

John Foster is the author of this book and the owner of **FOSTER'S TREE SERVICE**. I first heard of FOSTER'S on the **KTRH GardenLine** program hosted (then) by John Burrow and Bill Zak. Now that Bill has retired, Randy Lemmon is the co-host along with Burrow and they are still advertising FOSTER'S TREE SERVICE. In fact, both John Burrow and Randy Lemmon gave input in this text. They refer all callers who ask about trees to John Foster.

Rodney Rainey is an account executive for KTRH and one of his clients is Foster's Tree Service. A month or so ago Rodney called and asked if I'd publish a book written by John Foster about trees in and around Houston. I thought about it a minute and decided I'd rather have a book that could go *nationally,* because that's where the big bucks are, and told Rodney I'd think about it.

A few days passed and I received a call from John Foster who wanted to set up an appointment to discuss his book. We met at a restaurant midway for each of us. I had some free time and felt the least I could do was waste an hour or so and listen to the man. This is what I found.

As I talked with John, who was accompanied by

his 15-year-old son Johnathan, he told me why he was writing the book. "People who care about trees need to know about them and there is not a book that I've found that tells them the things I've learned."

"Oh, I've seen books that are 4 inches thick and in print so small that you need a magnifying glass to read, but written by someone who lives in New York or Washington who aren't familiar with *our* trees. I want my book to tell exactly how to plant and grow a tree in *this* area. I want to tell these tree owners about the trees that they *should* grow according to *these* soil conditions and climate, different here than any other place in the world! And, I want people to learn to care for their trees regardless of the kind they have."

He was sincere about the trees; I could tell. He added that he wasn't writing the book to make money or to promote his tree service; he has a thriving business. He wrote it for the trees.

I visited several more times with John Foster as he called on customers. His knowledge about trees dumfounded me, and the way he talked to his customers pleased me. I found, without doubt, that this book *will* educate you on caring for your trees. But it isn't for you; this book is for the trees! I hope you enjoy it.

Pete Billac
Editor and Publisher

ACKNOWLEDGMENTS

I could not have produced this book without the help of the following people who were willing to put their lives *on hold* as the book progressed.

PETE BILLAC, who put all the pieces together and helped me turn a bunch of words and ideas into a book I am proud of.

KENNY & ERIC GRAYSON, my field Arborists, who researched and studied to help me assure technical accuracy.

MARK EARLY & SELENA FOSTER, who typed, proofed, and edited most of the articles. And to **MS. CHAPIN,** my 9th grade English teacher.

And last but certainly not least, to my sweet and understanding wife **LISA**, who supported me even though for months, I spent more time with my computer than with her. She reads so much that she was given a perfect opportunity to critique each chapter. She also draws well; many of her illustrations are in this book.

There are more people to thank, but there isn't room to list them all; you know who you are and you know I'm indebted to you. Thank you.

TABLE OF CONTENTS

Part 2

Your Trees

Part I

UNDERSTANDING TREES

T rees furnish us with our prime necessities; wood for houses, food that we eat, shade to keep us cool, the furniture in our homes, rubber for the tires on our automobiles, and even toilet paper.

Think of all the items that we have come to truly need (or would rather not do without) that come from trees. Trees also help greatly in absorbing the noxious gases from many factories and convert it into oxygen. Scientists tell us that it takes many trees, per person, in order to maintain the carbon dioxide in atmospheric balance.

Protecting and maintaining healthy shade trees is a never-ending job that teaches you to truly respect nature. The forest is virtually a perfect environment for trees because of several factors that nature has provided.

First, the *underbrush* on the forest floor retains the fallen leaves and shelters them in a moist, cool humus environment that far surpasses any commercial composting system that we humans have yet to invent.

Secondly, trees are strong and healthy so they can physically *defend themselves* against diseases and insects.

And finally, when a forest tree dies there are hundreds more to take its place. If a tree falls from decay and crashes into another tree, it is considered the *natural order of things* and another tree replaces it.

Enter the human being and progress! We are appalled at the way our rain forests halfway around the world are being destroyed, and we spend billions of dollars trying to prevent this devastation. Yet we oftentimes neglect what is happening in our own back yard.

During construction of plants and factories, shopping centers and even our own homes, we introduce a bulldozer and backhoe to the land and destroy all but a token number of valuable trees. We take away their natural grade, rip out and expose roots, then go back and pile up fill dirt several inches high thereby *suffocating* already weakened root systems.

In addition, we pour concrete and wash out mortar mixers in the feeding areas of these trees thus adding dangerous levels of lime to the soil.

We don't *mean* to do these things. We aren't heartless or non-caring . . . just uninformed. What we've unconsciously done is make these wonders of nature mere potted plants encased between slabs, streets, and drives. To add to that bit of devastation, we then put in underground utilities crisscrossing through our yard and never stop to reason that the root system of these wondrous trees are within but *eighteen inches* of the surface. In Houston, with the clay soil, the roots are within *three to five inches* from the top of the ground. It happens like this as each minute passes, somewhere across the world.

Trees at Your New Home

The procedure usually goes like this in the case of a home buyer: You buy a new house because it suits your needs as far as space, location, afford ability, and perhaps because of the gorgeous trees located on the lot. Following the construction of your new home, you are content that the trees look so darn healthy and beautiful. All things considered, you are relieved that your trees have survived and can now take care of themselves. This, of course, is false!

At this point, the damage has been done. It is very difficult, sometimes impossible, to save trees once this has happened. My dad used to call it "trying to shut the gate after the cows get out." The trees have survived a hostile environment up until now. This is where the real work begins in improving the environment as much as possible.

This is where I come into your life with the information I plan to share with you in this book. If you follow what I'm about to tell you, your trees' chances of survival increase about a thousand percent. In reality, for the price of ten bucks, this book could save one, several, or all of your trees from an untimely death. And, being that I love trees so much, I'd rather have the few bucks now to help your trees survive in all their glory than to come out later, use my expertise and effort (and about $1,000 from your bank account, *per tree)* and still have only about a 50% chance of saving the tree. Care is everything!

Since you don't have the natural conditions of the forest which encourages tree growth you simply **must** get the proper amount of water, nutrition and aeration for that tree, or it weakens and increases its chances of dying. Oh, it would probably take a long time for that tree to die of neglect only, but this doesn't happen. By being weakened from neglect, *other things* kill it, such as disease or insects.

Then, a tree removal company is called in to cut it down, grind the stump, and it could cost (depending on the size and condition of the tree) another $1,000 —or more! Then, you spend an additional $1,500 to have a good landscaper plant a new tree. The difference in cost is astronomical as compared to trying to keep your tree healthy by doing it right in the first place. Yes, **care is everything!**

And, please, don't lull yourself into a false sense of security thinking that because the trees are large and mature that they will stay that way. Or that once they are grown, they can take care of themselves. And don't listen to the guy on TV who says that trees get fed when we feed the grass, because there isn't enough surface area to supply water and nutrients to a mature tree. Besides, grass food formula is different from the nutritional requirements a tree needs to maintain its optimum health, maybe survive.

I often drive down South Boulevard near Rice University in Houston, a place with tree-lined streets that is simply beautiful. There are Live Oaks that are perhaps 50 or 60 years old or older, and very tall. Many of them are dying and you can see where the older trees had been cut, the roots ground up and new trees planted. It always saddens me because it is nearing the end of an era when the area residents took care of their trees, and the trees tell the story without uttering a single word.

Most of the people in this fine residential area have lived here all their lives, and are at least as old as the trees. For perhaps the first twenty or thirty years, these Live Oaks needed nothing but a little water; they have a strong enough root system that in their early years they could have overcome just about anything.

I recall my dad telling me how he used to see the residents watering and supplying nutrients for these trees, but this hasn't happened nearly as often as it did back then. Now, the very same trees are stressed and dying. Back then, in the *old days*, they fertilized for $30 per tree per year using grass fertilizer. Today, we've learned that grass fertilizer simply isn't enough and the organic compounds and nutrients necessary to treat one typical front yard is about $520 for the first treatment, and $380 per year from then on.

And now, many of these trees still *seem* healthy, but many are not. The new residents think they have a healthy tree and most of the time it's difficult to tell (unless you're a professional) until it's too late. Many of these gorgeous, seemingly healthy trees have been neglected and stressed to the point that they are dying. Many, regardless of how much is spent, won't make it, and there are no guarantees when it comes to stressed trees.

I put in a memorial patio garden in front of the West University Place City Hall for my father, Ove Foster, who died in 1992. In that small portion of Houston that he loved so dearly, are some fine trees that are protected by one of the most comprehensive tree ordinances in the state. There is a bronze plaque to honor my father, and a ledge stone walkway surrounding an 18' Savannah Holly that the city of West University Place uses as their permanent Christmas tree for their yearly tree-lighting ceremony. My dad loved trees and he passed on that love to me. My life's work—as well as this book—are for **the trees** that I care about so fervently.

Preventing the Error

I know you've heard the axiom, "An ounce of prevention is worth a pound of cure." So, let's start with **building** a new home. Woefully, most builders know little about trees and even more could care less. They stick a tree in the yard where it looks nice, then leave. They might not put in a root barrier, they might plant the tree so that in four or five years it tears up your patio, causes the foundation of your house to crack or it is under some power lines or the tree dies.

As a small tree it looks good but let's look into the future. I would, without hesitation, **demand** that a *tree expert* look at these trees and not your builder; these are two distinct, specialized professions.

I've seen it so frequently when a new tree is not

planted properly and it might take six months to two years to die. But, it WILL die! The moment it was planted in that wrong area, its death knell sounded but you couldn't hear it because you didn't know what to listen for.

Most trees don't die of construction damage alone, but from secondary causes. The stress of construction damage weakens the tree thus inviting disease and insects. And your builder takes no responsibility for that tree. If you're smart, you'll pay that little extra at the beginning for a tree expert to help locate and plant your trees for you.

To give you an example of what can happen, the story I'm about to share with you is true. I'm not trying to frighten you to increase my business or that of any other tree professional, I simply care about trees and for those who take care of them.

I saw a beautiful house that cost about $150,000 to build. In six years, because a builder put in a tree with a large root system too near the house **without a root barrier**, the tree literally *drank* all the water from under the house and the foundation cracked! When the owner tried to sell the house, his lowest bid to repair the foundation was $40,000. Frightening, huh? The owner could either live there forever as it was and hope that the cracked foundation wouldn't cause his home to collapse or sell it at a tremendous loss. Yes, do it right the first time! Let me give you another example.

There was this other homeowner who had two 60-year-old oak trees growing in his yard and he was concerned over settling problems with the house; doors wouldn't shut. He saw cracks in the sheetrock. He called a foundation company who recommended and installed a root barrier which was right. What the foundation company did wrong, was the *method* they used to install the barrier. They did, in fact, protect the foundation from further damage, but in doing so they cut off about 30% of the root system.

Historically, foundation companies know from *nothing to very little* about trees. Most are not able to diagnose the damage they could cause by cutting off a tree's root system. They were also not knowledgeable enough to give the homeowner a proper treatment or watering program for the trees. It wasn't until **two years later** that the homeowner called me.

I wish I could tell you that I laid my hands on the trees and they were resurrected, but it just doesn't happen that way. It took another three years of costly treatment for both trees: one tree eventually died and the other cost a fortune to keep alive.

The moral of this story is to get a professional tree person (Arborist) to work along with the foundation company. It will cost a bit more but it will save the tree(s) and be done correctly. As the man on every TV and radio station in the city will tell you, do it the right way. It will, *Save You Money!*

Correcting the Error

More often than not, the degree of stress most trees are subjected to at a building site, with all that I mentioned above, causes their *immune system* to be suppressed and makes the tree defenseless against insects and disease invasion. Since their natural resources have been depleted, it is now our responsibility to *correct* some of the environmental problems we have created.

Woefully, you can't do it yourself. Or at least, call in a professional to *diagnose* the problem and then, perhaps you can do the rest yourself. Here is the procedure. We need to first . . .

Implement proper irrigation and watering

Correct the organic and nutrient levels in the soil

Integrate pest management

Periodical selective pruning

Monitor, assess and forecast

It is an established fact that trees growing in a city environment need to have a regular maintenance program because of the harsh conditions. The little bit of food and water they get usually comes from what we throw on the grass. Therefore, the only good conditions are within the first few inches from the top of the soil where the majority of the feeder roots grow.

A tree must have lots of water. When a tree runs out of water down deep, its roots come to the surface after surface water, usually stealing it from the grass which then causes the grass to die out and the area under the tree left barren. This is when you see exposed tree roots, the tree still searching for water. More often than not, it requires the advice of a trained professional who is familiar with *your particular area!*

Let me tell you some of the biggest headaches facing a tree expert in diagnosing tree problems today. From this, you can see that this book is for the trees as well as for your pocketbook or wallet. It takes a *trained professional!*

General Diagnosis

The biggest problem facing an arborist in diagnosing a tree, is the lack of available information. Unlike a medical doctor, the tree "doctor" cannot question the tree to describe the symptoms and since the history of the tree is of utmost importance, they must ask key questions to the homeowner about the site and the tree over the years. How long has this problem been going on? What were the early symptoms? Have there been any recent construction, excavation, or chemical treatments in this area? And the arborist knows that the information they receive isn't always accurate. The most common reply is, "It just seemed to have died overnight."

More often than not, the arborist is called in to treat the tree when it is either dying or dead and if you have the right answers, they might be able to save a dying tree but never can they resurrect a dead tree. They must follow these steps, and from what I'm telling you, you'll be able to spot an expert in minutes. Here's an example of what I mean.

I have a friend with a Mercedes who had a

problem with his automobile air conditioner not blowing cool air. Instead of taking the car to his Mercedes mechanic (a little out of his way and a bit more expensive), he stopped in a service station and asked a mechanic's *helper* to take a look, who put in a can of *Freon*. This fixed the problem *temporarily!* But in a week or so it was blowing warm again.

When the professional Mercedes mechanic finally got the car, he discovered that the damage done by adding Freon without a single drop of oil caused everything to go awry. The system overheated, the exhaust fan stopped and the compressor needed replacing. Final cost was $2,387, which means if you want it done correctly, go to a professional. It will save you much money and strife.

I know, this story seems to have nothing to do with trees, but it does! First, I'm advising you to call a professional, and next, I'm going to tell you how to spot someone who knows little or nothing about your tree problem so you can, as quickly as possible, make some lame excuse and say you'll call them back and never call them again. Whatever you choose to do or say, I don't care, just as long as you bid them goodby and get them as far away from this precious (maybe) live tree before they kill it. Here is what a professional will do.

Step 1. They have to accurately identify the tree.

There are many insects and diseases that are specific to certain host trees. Knowing the identity of the tree can quickly limit the number of suspected causes.

Step 2. They must look for a pattern or abnormality.

An arborist must first know what is normal for that tree. For example, when some species of pines shed their interior needles in the spring, some homeowners think their trees are dying; they are not! An arborist will compare that tree to other trees on that site. Uniform damage over a large area (even different species of trees) usually indicates nonliving factors such as physical injury, chemicals, weather, etc. Non-uniform damage patterns can be indicative of living factors such as insects or pathogens.

Step 3. Carefully examine the site.

They will check the contour of the land and note the structures present. If an affected tree is restricted to a walkway, road or fence, the disorder could be a result of wood preservatives or other harsh chemicals.

The history of property may reveal grade changes, excavations, herbicide applications, or gas leaks. They must look at the community where the tree is located. How do other trees look of the same species? Is the area a new community with imported plants or trees not native to the area? Is it an older community where age and over crowding can be limiting factors? Or is it a new housing division in an old wooded lot?

Step 4. Note the color, size and thickness of the foliage.

Dead leaves at the top of the tree are usually the result of mechanical or environmental root stress. Twisted or curled leaves may indicate viral infection, insect feeding, or exposure to herbicides. Early fall color can be a sign of girdling roots or other root related problems.

Step 5. Check the trunk and branches.

Examine the trunk thoroughly for wounds because wounds provide entrances for canker and wood-rotting organisms. Small holes may indicate the presence of borers or bark beetles.

Step 6. Examine the roots.

They must note the color of the roots. Healthy, fibrous roots are generally white and fleshy. Brown roots may indicate dry soil conditions or the presence of toxic chemicals. Black roots often reflect overly wet soil or the presence of root-rotting organisms.

I don't mean to *throw* all these problems at you at once but these give you an idea of what a tree expert must look for and if they don't seem to be looking for these things, ask them what they are doing. If they don't do all or most of these things when inspecting your tree, "drive off" so to speak, and call someone else.

A qualified arborist will begin diagnosing a tree problem *systematically* in order to rule out certain possibilities. The majority of tree problems are *not* possibilities. The majority of tree problems are *not* caused by insects, mites, fungi or bacteria; 70-90% are the results of adverse cultural and environmental conditions such as soil compaction, drought, moisture fluctuation, temperature extremes, mechanical injuries, or poor species selection. This is why, later on in this book, I list the **best** trees for this area. Trees, to me, are like kids; I love them all but different ones need different conditions and different treatment for them to be healthy and happy.

Symptoms & Signs

I'd prefer you not do this diagnosis yourself; it really is something that takes a trained eye. It is difficult for an untrained person to detect symptoms or effects of an injury on a tree that are apparent to an arborist. Examples include chlorosis, wilting, and leaf scorch. In chlorosis, leaves yellow with veins remaining green. You can easily recognize a leaf that has wilted.

Rarely can a problem be diagnosed by a single symptom. Usually, a person with a tree problem takes a leaf into their local nursery and asks about the problem. All that nurseryman can do is tell them what the problem is with *that particular leaf*, but an arborist, to properly diagnose the problem, has to look at the *entire tree!*

Wilting can be the result of drought, root problems, or various fungal or bacteria organisms. Signs might include insect frass (droppings—could be debris or sawdust, "things" that denotes the presence of insects), emergence holes, or discarded skins.

Nine out of ten times when I go out to look at a tree, the symptoms that frightened the tree owner have very little to do with what is actually wrong with the tree. I see trees with leaves *half* the size they should be. Perhaps the foliage is thinner at the top than it is on the rest of the tree. I might see surface roots all over the place, or rough bark on a typically smooth bark tree. The combination of all this represents a tree that has been suffering from environmental problems for years. It is so weak that a single attack of borers could kill it. You just **cannot** perform the proper diagnosis on an entire tree simply from looking at one leaf.

One problem that I confront four out of five times daily is when I get a call from someone wanting their trees pruned. I look at the tree and find all of the symptoms described above. When I tell the people that their tree needs an extensive root treatment program, some think I'm trying to bump them up in price; their call was for me to *prune* their tree and they don't want to hear all that I have to say, they just want a price on pruning.

It is far **cheaper** to *treat and save* the tree than it is to have it pruned. I suggest they wait on the pruning and let's get their tree healthy again.

Pictured on the next page are six of the most common tree ailment symptoms and how they affect the leaves.

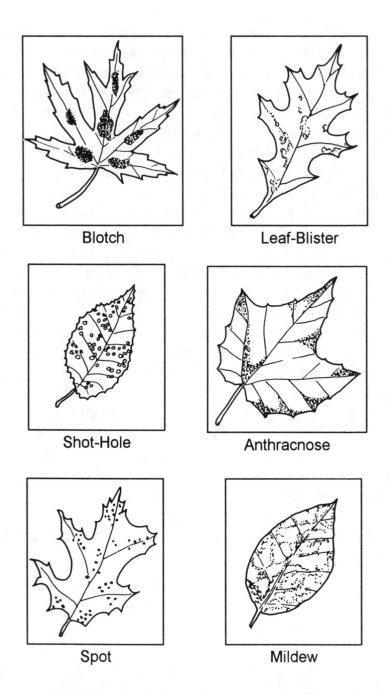

Blotch

Leaf-Blister

Shot-Hole

Anthracnose

Spot

Mildew

If your tree has but a few leaf spots, pick off the infected leaves. If it's severe, try spraying with a fungicide containing maneb chlorothalonil *(Daconil 2787) captan (Orthocide) or zineb Daconisyplant.* You can find these at most full-service nurseries.

Doing It Yourself

I didn't write this book to make money, nor did I do it to advertise my tree service; I *give it* to my clients who have been working very hard to maintain their trees over the years, people who care enough about their trees to be out there in the yard on weekends, making things happen.

If you found this book in a retail store or heard about it over the radio, I hope it tells you enough about trees to be able to care for them yourself, or convinces you to call in a tree expert if you suspect any problems: "And ounce of prevention really is worth a pound of cure" in this instance. Now, if you *do* plan to do it yourself, here's how.

Proper Watering

The single most important factor for the health of any tree is **water!** *Deep* watering is important and, mature trees need hundreds of gallons of water each day! In order to tell you how long to water, it's necessary that you know the type of soil where you live. If it's clay, you may need to water in cycles with a sprinkler system of 10 minutes per section per hour and run it three cycles. Or, one 20-minute cycle if your soil is sandy loam. The trick is to get water down deep.

Sand	1 inch of water penetrates up to 12 inches
Loam	1 inch of water penetrates 6 to 10 inches
Clay	1 inch of water penetrates 4 to 5 inches

I took my publisher with me today to give him an idea about trees so he can understand what I do and why I'm writing this book. We looked at one tree, a Live Oak, that was planted in a section of Houston that was heavy in clay. This tree needed **deep root watering.**

The *drip line* of the tree (outside the umbrella of branches) is where these roots must be watered. In many parts of Houston we have a compacted clay soil that we call **gumbo** that is difficult to penetrate. A few years ago I figured out an answer for this that has proven highly successful.

One day I got a call from a lady in Lake Jackson who had a Live Oak tree that was a couple of hundred years old in her back yard. She built a new house about 25 feet from this majestic old tree. Half the tree died almost overnight and she called me.

Now, I rarely to never do any work that far away from the small section of Houston where I spend most of my time; it is just not cost effective. But, after the lady described the tree, I just had to see it and do what I could to save it.

Just as she told me, the tree was nearly dead. She agreed that I should begin treating it to try and save it. The reality was that it was almost impossible to stay on that kind of regular program, year after year, because of the expense of having a professional drive miles from Houston to do it. I had to figure out a way to save the tree and do it with a minimal cash output for the lady.

I talked to this lady's grandson who was willing to spend a few weekends digging holes with the auger on his tractor. He saved his grandmother's tree by using my plan. Here is what I told him to do and this is what you can do!

With a post hole digger, make holes 18 inches deep and as wide (or a bit wider) than your post hole digger. Then, fill the holes with rocks (not gravel, but large rocks) ranging from ¾" to 1½" in diameter. Make these holes about 10' apart in a sort of grid system throughout the yard. That's it! And every time you turn on the sprinkler system or water with a hose or it rains, the water fills these holes and eventually spreads out and you get aeration. The part of the yard that got too much water now drains.

I originally got this idea at the age of 14 when I was in Rayford Kay's office, who was the Harris County Agricultural Extension Agent at the time. I discovered a pamphlet describing a variation of a *French Drain System*. Years later, while visiting this lady from Lake Jackson, I remembered that French Drain System and incorporated it into my own deep-watering system.

This procedure also helps reduce foundation problems. The tree will have other places to get water besides it's favorite place—under your house! And, if you to fill the last few inches of the hole with mulch so that the grass will grow over it, nobody knows the rock-filled holes are there except you . . . and the healthy, happy tree!

Just a few days ago I received a letter from Barbara Day at Hampton Gardens Landscaping, who told me that she has had great results from the trees she used this method on. So, if you can't do it yourself, call Hampton Gardens.

Organic Materials & Nutrients

Periodically, it becomes necessary to *help trees along* by adding additional organic compounds and nutrients to the soil and root systems to build up stressed or weak trees or even to maintain the good health of a healthy *looking* tree.

I refer to this system as *Deep Root Treatment* instead of *fertilizing* or *feeding.* You see, in the Houston area, excessive nitrogen is unnecessary, even detrimental, to tree health because of the subtropical weather we have. Most "tree fertilizer" in this country is designed for trees in colder climates where trees are top stressed. The focus in those areas is to supplement the crown.

In contrast, we live in an area where the trees are **root** stressed. Our trees don't have enough root system to support the crown in the first place.

Supplementing the crown on our trees would merely overload an already strained root system.

Also, most commercial fertilizers have a high salt content which tends to have a detrimental effect on the microbes that help convert the raw organics to a usable form and *fertilizing* means adding **nitrogen** to them. I also know from experience that nitrogen is harmful because it *activates the fungi* that are damaging to the root systems.

I hope I'm not getting too technical and that I've not lost some of you readers. I don't mean to insult you but as I read over this I can see where I might be writing things you don't care about. Still, I plan to continue because I want you to care about these trees and if you don't understand any part of this, call me and I'll do my best to explain it to you—no charge!

Summer Supplements

When we have a hot summer in Houston (like most of the time), our trees suffer from more stress than usual, especially in August, near the end of summer. I must caution you to leave this summer fertilizing to the professionals. The wrong formulations can cause serious trouble.

ANTHRACNOSE . . .

Trees become weak for many reasons; one prime example is anthracnose. A disease causing lesions or necrotic spots that can affect the stem, leaf or fruit of a tree. Most shade trees in this area are susceptible to anthracnose. To detect it, look for small irregular spots formed along the edge of the leaf or along the veins in that leaf. As it gets worse, the leaves fall off prematurely. The good part of this is that anthracnose rarely kills. It defoliates a tree. But, if a tree is defoliated every year it becomes stressed and thus susceptible to other problems.

There is **no cure** for anthracnose, but it can be controlled. The recommended spray program is not very cost-effective for trees because the spray lasts but a few weeks, and for large trees a professional must do the work. Also, trees that are too weak to fight off this fungus on their own will have it back the following year, spray or not.

Therefore, just get the tree back to good health and the tree will control the disease. If the conditions are right, the tree can utilize the minerals already in the soil (copper, zinc, manganese). These minerals are the natural fungicides that the trees have always used. A good example is copper. Products like *Daconil* and *Kocide 101* are copper-based fungicides that cost a fortune to buy and apply. It can be used on bedding plants, but having a professional come out and spray gallons of it on a mature tree every time it wears off, who can afford it?

O AK WILT . . .
                        Oak Wilt is a disease caused by a fungus that is spread from tree to tree by insects, grafted (intertwined) roots, and tools that are not

sterilized. This fungus spreads through the water-conducting vessels in the wood, causing the discoloration and plugging. The leaves then begin to wilt, and the branches—or the entire tree—dies.

Right now, Oak Wilt is almost nonexistent in Houston (2 trees in Pasadena have been diagnosed with it, but they are isolated in a field) and it is still in the Hill Country. The way Oak Wilt will come here is through *firewood* brought in from the Hill Country. Beetles carrying the fungal spores of Oak Wilt on their legs will walk across fresh, open cuts where Oak trees have been pruned (and not painted over) and the fresh cut veins of an untreated cut will suck the spores into the tree.

The only physical barrier to keep these beetles from the open wound could be a simple tree spray paint. It only has to last for a couple of days because in a few days the wound will suberize (form a transparent coating over these veins).

B ORERS ...

Look for these rascals. They are the #1 killers of hardwoods in Harris County. These tiny critters can infect even the healthiest of trees. The most likely times are when the trees are stressed from the constant weather changes we have to endure.

There are hundreds of kinds of borers (borers are the larvae of flying insects that burrows into trees or wood). Most homeowners who talk about borers mean *dry wood borers*, the ones that make big holes in an old wooden post. If you have these big holes in your tree, it means that these borers have found soft, dry wood. In short, the tree has bigger problems than borers. It means that all the veins in that part of the tree have collapsed and the borers are going after the wood. The tree is in danger of falling down.

Sometimes you will see black resin weeping from a pencil-sized hole. You won't see the borers, so there's no need to show you a picture or drawing of one, just look for the evidence. Usually, when you *see* this evidence, it's too late to do anything about it and your tree is dying. The only *possible* alternative is to inject the trunk with an insecticide every few months and try to nurse it back to health. Your other choices are to have it cut down now, or wait for it to die.

Now, we get down to the big bad boy himself, the **Shothole Borer,** so named because the size of the holes (like birdshot) are so small that chances are high that you'll never find them. In most cases the tree is already dead by the time these borers are detected. Also, if you should see a whitish yellow sawdust at the base of the tree, the tree is gone and it's just a matter of time before it falls. **Have it cut down now!**

Three to four weeks after the tree is dead, the leaves turn brown but remain on the tree. To prevent borers from invading a tree, the best thing to do is to keep the tree healthy, which includes watering and deep root treatment. Infestation of borers requires *prayer* more than anything. You can try trunk injections but this will probably not help. **Keeping** the tree healthy is your only defense. An ounce of prevention truly IS worth a pound of cure.

S AP SUCKERS . . .

As delightful a cartoon character as he is, Woody Woodpecker is an unwanted bird to have around. Not only is there this constant pecking noise but if you look in your tree and see rows of parallel holes about ¼ inch diameter on the trunk, perhaps with sap oozing from these holes and portions of the surrounding bark falling off, you'll probably see yellow-breasted or red-breasted birds pecking away at the tree.

There are two different species of sapsuckers, members of the woodpecker family. They search for a tree with a high sugar content and when they find it, they visit it many times a day and come back to feed on it year after year.

After a certain number of holes, the bark falls off and the tree above the damaged area dies. Oftentimes, disease organisms enter these holes, do extensive damage or perhaps kill the entire tree.

You can try *wrapping* the damaged trunk with burlap or smearing a sticky material (such as latex used for ant control) above and below this line of holes to inhibit the pecking damage.

The trees in this area that are commonly damaged by sapsuckers are Pines, Fir, Red and Sugar Maple, Silk Oak, Palms and Willow.

S LIME FLUX . . .

Slime Flux (Wetwood) attack the

trunk, roots and branches of a tree. It is a bacteria that infects a tree during water soaked conditions of wood. This part of the wood is dead and is usually discolored and contains fatty acids that give it a sour or rancid odor. This liquid supports the growth of many other kinds of bacteria, yeasts, and fungi that give it a slime texture and often fetid color and odor. This foul brew, which may bubble at a wound, is unsightly but doesn't really hurt anything. There may be some wilting on affected branches and it does draw insects.

The best method I've found to combat Slime Flux is to wash the affected areas with a water/clorox mixture or use *Consan Triple Action 20* as directed on the label. Most of the time, it will simply go away on its own.

LEAF SPOT . . .

No need to worry, Leaf Spot does little damage and it's difficult to prevent anyway. What happens is that fungal spores flying through the air start in a small spot and expand. It's almost impossible to know when this (*phyllostica)* will be active, so preventive fungicide is a *hit and miss* proposition. But, an owner of a magnolia tree sees these spots and it concerns them.

If there are but a few leaves like this, pick them off and burn them. If you can spray, try *Daconil 2787*, or *Captan* (Orthocide) or *Zineb*.

GALLS, TUMORS & CANKERS . . .

I get many calls about leaf gall which is not harmful to trees. The most common is *Wooly Oak Gall*, a yellow fuzzy thing that gets all over the leaves of Live Oaks. It happens like this.

A wasp lays her eggs in these spots and the stimulation of her stinger on the leaf tissue causes this reaction. Just bag the leaves and throw them away.

Stem Gall acts the same way. These are the little round balls that infect the stems of Live Oaks. Don't worry about it either. But, be aware that if this gall is on the *main branches* of your tree—or trunk or roots, this may present a problem. A gall in this area is referred to as a Canker or Tumor.

Cankers (Tumors) can be bacterial, fungal, or insect related. It is very important to know which you are dealing with because most cankers are similar to human cancer; as the canker grows it monopolizes space. Cells that don't benefit the tree collapse the vascular systems, and this is the time to call in a professional. Early detection is the key. There are far too many cankers to list. If you see what *looks like* one and it's on the branches, trunk or roots of your tree, make that call now.

MYCORRHIZAE . . .

is a product applied to tree roots that helps the tree find water in a hostile environment (such as the city). Mycorrhizae (*fungus root)* is an absorbing organ composed of both root and fungal cells where the roots and the fungus get together and form one united organism that help the tree deal with this hostile environment.

It has taken our company almost 30 years to find a product that gives us anything even *close* to the results that my father's original formulations produced. Our staff at Foster's has done extensive field testing on the product. We found that areas where Mycorrhizae was applied proved to have an almost 100% better response than if we applied water alone. Then, when we used our root treatment formulas **and** Mycorrhizae, we nearly doubled the success of using Mycorrhizae alone.

DAMAGE FROM LIGHTNING . . .

is extensive to trees; most lightning-struck trees do not survive because of root damage and damage to the vascular system. Lightning causes many forest fires. This is how lightning produces such awesome devastation.

When a tree is struck by lightning, the force almost **rips it out of the ground!** The lightning charge follows the water in a tree that grounds out at the microscopic root hairs that literally explode! Then, the intensified charge goes **back** up the veins of the tree, tearing off bark all the way up. This charge can go up and down like this **2 to 20 times** in less than a second.

A high proportion of trees struck by lightning

eventually die either because of the injury to the tree itself, or the *opportunistic organisms* the dead wood attracts. This is why lightning-struck pine trees are usually a lost cause. It is difficult for a tree to repair damage this critical before insects invade it or disease sets in.

Beetles usually attack within 48 hours of a lightning strike; they can smell the turpentine from blocks away. The "bleeding" of the tree draws them and since we don't have enough freezes in a Houston winter to harden the sap, the tree can bleed for years. Trees that do survive a lightning strike may develop various abnormalities, usually disfigured by death of limbs of the top of the tree.

To prevent a lightning strike, lightning rods are installed on valuable trees, with copper cables leading down the trunk and through the soil to grounding rods driven into soil beyond the branch spread of the tree.

Trees in this area mostly struck by lightning are Ash, Tulip, Pine, Oak and Elm. Actually, no species is totally immune. Location and size of the tree are also factors that influence susceptibility.

Golfers, usually when there is rain, there's lightning, put your club in your bag and scamper to the clubhouse. It could save your life or at the very least, keep you dry.

 **ALL MOSS . . .**

(a.k.a. Bunch Moss) is an

Epiphyte, which is a photosynthetic plant that grows upon other plants. It usually attaches itself to the bark of a tree (twigs, wires, poles and even chain link fence) by means of a root or rhizomes, gaining support from the tree but not necessarily parasyzing it.

Ball Moss appears as gray-green tufts that develop into dense clusters composed of numerous individual plants. Its stems are branched but short, and the ash-colored to reddish leaves grow to lengths of about 5 centimeters. When it grows on rough bark, it produces rootlike hold fasts for attachment.

Ball Moss can be detrimental to the tree. The universities will tell you that it's not an organism that hurts trees, but *I'm* telling you that Ball Moss, because of its propensity to *wrap around* the limb, tends to cut off the circulation of the limb as it grows. When this happens, it weakens the limbs and could possibly kill it. To rid your tree of Ball Moss, spray in May or June with a copper-base fungicide (Kocide 101 that you get at any lawn and garden store) and follow the directions on the label.

Most oak trees have what is known as *Spanish Moss* and, like Ball Moss, live off moisture in the air. If your Spanish Moss gets thick enough, It restricts the sunlight from getting to the leaves. When you have your tree pruned, have them thin out the Spanish Moss. Your tree service company will know how.

If you want to do it yourself, pull it out, knock it out with a large stick or get a long pole saw (8 feet long with 8-foot extensions). Mostly though, the moss is so high that it can be dangerous to climb the tree yourself. You have to call out a tree company.

It's easy to tell the difference between Spanish Moss and Ball Moss; one hangs and the other wraps.

M ISTLETOE . . .

is a parasitic evergreen plant with small yellowish-green leaves, yellowish flowers, and waxy white berries, growing on the branches of certain trees, oaks in particular. Men love it at Christmas time, especially when they hang it over a doorway and kiss all the lovely ladies who walk under it.

Mistletoe roots into the tree and saps nutrients from the tree without replacing them. Eventually, the tree is supporting the mistletoe and not itself and can end up dying. It can be controlled by cutting it out but since it is rooted in the tree, it keeps coming back. There are studies being made to chemically control mistletoe.

Trunk Injection

We have had excellent results using a unique system for treating severely stressed trees. This technique consists of microencapsulated nutrients and pesticides that are directly injected into the root flares of the tree (where the roots begin to flare out at the trunk) and the nutrients bypass the root system and go straight to the vascular system. It works on the same principle as the IV's in a human.

Trunk Injecting has taken a "bad rap" lately because do-it-yourselfers can now buy these capsules themselves and then do it incorrectly. Follow the directions on the label. If the label doesn't tell you *where,* simply drill at the base of the tree and put this pressurized canister in the hole.

The problem is in **diagnosis**, and most people don't know how to assess what trees need. Injection can be useless, or it can cause serious problems for the tree. If the tree has a bacterial disease the injection of streptomycin sounds good, but the antibiotic is suspended in fertilizer, and fertilizer activates bacteria.

This is a quick fix and goes away in no time.

Bacterial Diseases

Bacteria are microscopic organisms that are neither plant nor animal; they do not have an organized, well-drained cell nucleus like plant and animal cells. Most bacteria live on decaying organic matter. About 200 species of bacteria cause plant diseases.

Bacteria vary in their ability to survive in the soil without a host; some can live and multiply in the soil, while others die off. They damage plants by causing leaf spots, soft rots, blights, wilts, galls and cankers. Bacteria often live within a protective *ooze* that they produce on infected plant parts. When conditions are warm and moist, this ooze, containing millions of bacteria, is exuded by infected plants. Infection spreads when this ooze is splashed to healthy plant parts or other plants, and when bacteria are transferred from diseased plants to healthy plants by contaminated hands, tools, or insects.

CONTROL: Bacterial diseases are more difficult to control than fungal diseases. The available chemicals such as *streptomycin* or *basic copper sulfate*, are not very effective, but when used in combination with good sanitation, can usually keep infection to a minimum. When possible, use resistant plant varieties.

Pine Bark Beetle

A Pine Bark Beetle can kill your pine tree *before* you know it's even there! One method I'd use, is to keep an eye out on pine trees *in your neighborhood* and if one is about to succumb to "tree heaven" look closely at your own tree and either spray it or have us come out and look at it.

Pine Bark Beetles usually attack weak trees. Any chemical the EPA allows you to spray on a tree will be biodegradable and gone in less than a month. Beetles, though most prevalent in the hotter months, can hit any time of year. Not only is this chemical bad for the environment but it isn't practical to spend $100+ per month per tree. By the time you recognize signs of beetles in a tree, in most cases the tree is dead already, it just hasn't turned brown yet—but it will!

SOLUTION: Keep trees healthy and **prevent** these invaders from destroying your trees. By providing the trees with a better environment, i.e., proper food and water, they will eventually gain the strength to fend off these insects.

Something for the future that universities and laboratories are working on (hasn't been developed yet) is a *Pheromone* they will perhaps inject a tree with or maybe hang in a tree in a bag that **prevents** these pine bark beetles from attacking a tree.

You see, a Pine Bark Beetle will not attack a tree that is dead because there isn't any of this delicious turpentine for them to feed from. Pine Bark Beetles attack weakened trees and eventually kill them! When the beetles leave, they emit a smell (Pheromone). So, if scientists can duplicate the scent, they can fool the attacking beetles into believing a healthy tree is dead, thus saving the tree from infestation.

Of course, this means people who **don't treat their trees** and keep them healthy or who aren't aware of this Pheromone they can use, will get more beetles.

Pruning

If you don't know what you're doing, please don't try it. There is but one way to prune your tree and I'll tell you how it's done. You prune your tree for several reasons:

✔To cut away the dead branches because you're afraid they might fall and hurt someone;

✔To get them away from the roof of your house to prevent them from damaging your roof in high winds, or to prevent limbs from scraping keeping you awake at night or so the leaves won't clog up your drains;

✔To improve the appearance of the tree;

✔To allow the sun to pass through so your grass under the tree canopy will grow;

✔Because you want it to grow taller or wider;

✔To reduce wind resistance (strong winds will catch these leaves like sails, cause them to sway, weaken, and maybe break, thus damaging the tree);

✔For general tree health. If a tree is too dense, it prevents the sunlight from coming in and prevents the inner leaves (those in constant shade) from producing photosynthesis, the process the tree uses to manufacture food;

✔To compensate for a weak root system or loss of a root system.

Tree pruning can be healthy for the tree under the right circumstances; it can also be harmful. The International Society of Arboculture has set standards that are helpful. This is a good place to start if you don't have anyone you trust to care for your trees.

How and when and whether you prune at all depends on the tree. With a Live Oak for example, cutting large branches is not advisable. Live Oaks are, traditionally, short, squatty trees and will not grow tall.

If you cut large branches off, the remainder of the tree will grow thicker and bushier but, no taller. That's why **knowing** what tree to plant is the smart way to go.

You see, when a large branch is cut from any tree, all of the leaves that were growing on it are replaced by the tree somewhere else on that tree. The tree automatically does it! Take off a large branch and the leaves densely grow back on what's left of the tree, thus causing the tree to be pruned more often, it creates a greater danger of limbs being broken in a high wind, and more sunlight is blocked from plants and grass that you might want to grow under that tree.

That's why, in most instances, the more places the leaves have to grow the better the leaf distribution, and you have a tree with a balanced canopy that is healthier, more attractive, and safer.

However, I know you don't want limbs slapping you in the face as you try to mow under the tree. Nor do you want tree limbs scraping against your roof disturbing you or raking shingles off onto the lawn. So this is how it's done.

Let the tree spread out. Most trees have limbs with downward and upward growing forks. You can train them by **cutting** the downward growing forks and leave the upward growing forks growing up and out.

I get many calls from people who ask me to trim the heavy branches off their particular tree because "It's rubbing against the house. See?" That's the fault of two people; the builder who knew nothing about planting a tree and just wanted it to look good where it was in order to sell the house. And **you,** because you didn't know the questions to ask until it was too late to prevent this from happening. By reading this book, you not only know what you did wrong but now, how to do it correctly.

I make it a point to trim the branches that are disturbing you by scraping against the roof, and leave the ones that are 6 or so feet above the roof because these branches provide a sort of cushion in the event the higher and heavier branches break.

You see, if a branch that is 6 feet away breaks in a high wind or rain, chances are only the leafy part will slap against the roof and cause little damage. If it is cut away, the rest of the tree will develop extra-heavy leaf growth (to compensate itself from this branch loss) thus making it less wind resistant. Then, if an **upper** limb breaks in a high wind or rainstorm and the lower branch has been cut, it has a strong chance of going **through** the roof.

If you want to prune your own tree, go to **every part of that tree** and cut every **third** limb that is **finger-sized,** thereby effectively removing 33% of the growth without disturbing the natural distribution of limbs.

The tools to use in pruning are a sharp saw or clippers.

All cutting instruments should be sterilized by dipping them in ½ Clorox and ½ water between trees to prevent the spread of disease. In the case of already diseased trees such as pear trees with fire blight, the cutting instrument has to be sterilized between *cuts.* If not, the cutting instrument will spread these bacteria.

There is so much to know about pruning trees

that it would take almost an entire book to tell you how to do it correctly. I hate to sound like a broken record by saying "call a tree company" but it truly is your wisest choice. However, if you want to do it yourself, here are some standard rules.

❶Whichever branches you'd *like* to prune and you're determined to do it yourself, and assuming that you can reach these branches with relative ease, first, I urge you to be careful. Make certain that the ladder you plan to use is sound and if you lean it against the trunk of the tree and plan to lean out, use a safety belt and rope; it's just too easy to lose your balance and fall.

❷Get a sharp saw to do the work. You can use a chain saw (if you must) but I'd prefer you use a sharp hand saw. There are a variety of those at your lawn and garden store.

If you're thinning, remember, cut every third branch and as close to the large limb as you can. To be certain, dab or spray that cut with tree paint. I don't think it's necessary but it looks good and the cost is only a few cents per squirt or dab. Better yet, look in the **Ortho Tree Pruning** book found at most nurseries for additional and/or up-to-date information. If you plan to cut a large limb, use this diagram as a guide. You see, if you make but a single cut, the weight of the branch will tear out parts of the trunk. If you make that first cut a foot **from** the trunk, from *underneath*, and a second one 2 to 4" above that, the limb falls and leaves just a stub. So, your 3rd cut is the stub (cut ¼" from the trunk), put tree paint on it and it's done.

The danger in this is rarely the damage *you'll* do to the tree if you follow my cutting and paint procedure.

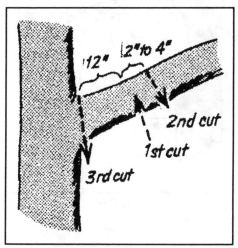

Notch Branch

For instance, if the tree is large and you place your ladder against a broad part of the trunk, it's difficult to reach around to cut the branch; you'll have to get on the side of the trunk where the branch might fall, either swatting you down from your perch like a fly or knocking the ladder out from under you. This is yet another reason to call in a professional. A tree limb is less expensive to have cut that the doctor bill if you break one of your own limbs.

❸Now, once you've cut these limbs, it's time to seal the wound with pruning paint or wound dressing. You can get this in a spray can at any full-service nursery, perhaps even smaller lawn and garden shops.

Ever since I can recall, Texas A&M has changed

their standard on painting tree wounds. Currently I agree with their recommendation: you must paint fresh cuts on all oak trees to prevent the spread of Oak Wilt.

My thought on tree paint is that you paint **all** wounds larger than a half dollar. Use a tree paint rather than creosote, roofing tar, or something toxic to the tree. I say use tree paint all the time. I can't swear that it helps the healing process, but when you have

Seal Cuts

an open wound on a limb, the exposed wood is more prone to accept moisture from the air and it promotes tree rot. If rot begins, it makes the scar tissue more difficult to heal over this untreated and exposed area.

❹Especially during hurricane seasons when the winds begin to blow hard, tree limbs break and could cause damage to your home or to the tree. Have the trees pruned back *before* the hurricane season to lessen the wind resistance.

You can do it yourself but we don't recommend it. It gets mighty scary 20, 30 or so feet up in a tree and few people have ladders that reach that high. On shorter cuts up to 20 feet with a ladder that does reach, it's happened where some people put the ladder **after** the cut and came tumbling down. And others lean the topmost part of their ladder on the branch *before* the cut, and when they cut the **outer part** of the limb off, what happens? The weight is gone, so the tree limb supporting your ladder **rises** and you and the ladder come plummeting down. Get a tree trimming company to do it for you!

> If you'll take note, not many professional tree companies even *own* a ladder; ladders are not made to fit against a rounded tree trunk.

Most of the tree trimming companies have ropes and saddles to hoist themselves in the tree to do the work, and the ones who do the trimming are athletic. It is hard work that requires extreme physical strength.

Tree Removal

If you have a dead tree in your yard or some scary limbs in a healthy tree that look menacingly weak, call a tree service to get them down *before* the hurricane season. Get them out of there *before* they cause major damage and remember, if you **do** plan to do it yourself, be extremely careful.

On the day I took my publisher with me, we went to one place for a tree removal job, the charge was $285. We went to another, the tree there was about 3 times the size and the charge was $740. He wanted to know why the vast difference in price. Let me explain it to you.

Each tree removal is different; rarely are two jobs exactly the same. Personally, I tend to either **break even or lose money** on tree removals; I do it as a service to my customers and hope I get referrals to *save*, *maintain*, and *prune* trees, the principal function of my business.

Situation #1—Cut down a tree for $285

I sent out a crew of 4 men. This particular tree was a Chinese Tallow, maybe 30 feet high and had three trunks, each about 10" in diameter. It was growing in a small patio and leaning against a garage. To get to it we could drive the truck next to the garage, stand on the garage roof that was solid, and reach the top portion with ropes and climbing gear.

We then cut the top branches which we could toss over the garage right onto the truck, then work down. When we got to the main trunks, we could work from the patio and we cut it ground level and left the stump. It was easy. For that (and since the crew was already there to prune another tree), the cost was less.

Situation #2—Cut down the tree for $740

This tree, a very large and old Chinese

Tallow, was maybe 70 feet high with a trunk of about 3' in diameter. It had many large branches, each about the size of one trunk of the smaller tree I talked about above. To get to it we had to walk, carrying the cut limbs and trunk maybe 90 to 100 feet to the waiting truck. Also, it was leaning over the neighbor's fence on two sides and was growing around power lines. The garage next to it couldn't be used because the roof was old and weak.

*It would take my 4-man crew about **6 hours** to complete this job and then, only if the owner got permission from their neighbors for us to go into these other two back yards. If permission wasn't given, it would take my crew all of **two days** to do the job and hence, the price would more than triple and yet, we still lose money!*

So, for you to get an *accurate bid* on tree removal, it is necessary that the tree company come out and make an **onsite** appraisal. And, other than what most people believe, a **dead tree** cost more to remove than a dying or live one. A dead tree crumbles, breaks, and is very dangerous to climb.

While driving from this job-estimate and talking with my publisher, he asked a myriad of questions. "I guess you make a lot of money after a wind storm or hurricane?"

"I **lose** money," I answered quickly. "The last big hurricane we had in Houston, no less than forty new tree-removal companies appeared. Everyone who had a pickup truck and a chain saw became a **tree expert** overnight! They messed up more often than not, but they were cheap! They destroyed trees that could have been saved. In trimming, they cut off main branches, untreated, and left the tree standing, not knowing they had killed it. They had trees fall on roof tops, power lines, a neighbor's fence, a car or two, their own truck and on themselves. They didn't have any insurance and the homeowner "bit the bullet." As a result, we have a host of homeowners who now hate or at least, have great disdain for all tree companies. My business suffers every time there is a natural disaster."

I hope you've learned a bit about the importance of trees and how to care for them. I don't mean to use scare tactics with you on their care and if you can read this book and find out how to care for them yourself, I've done my job. If you aren't certain, call a tree expert to help. Now, let's go into the specific trees that grow easiest and healthiest in Houston.

Part 2

YOUR TREES

One of the few questions I can't answer is when someone asks me, "What is the best tree to plant in my yard?" I can't tell them that any more than I can tell them if the person their son or daughter is engaged to is the best person for them to marry. Here's the way I have to answer that question.

First, if they know a particular tree they think they'd *like* to have, I give them information on that particular tree such as how high, how long, how much, etc. What I'd like them to do is to read this book and select a particular tree(s) that they like best *after* they know what the tree can do for them.

And this isn't difficult, because there are only 8 or 10 trees that grow well in Houston, and maybe only 4 or 5 that should be planted in a certain **section** of this area.

If you don't have a particular tree in mind, I'd still ask them to read what I have to say about various trees and then decide which to plant. See how easy it is to make the right decision and avoid costly mistakes?

Let me caution you on what I think it best **not** to do after you read what I have to say about trees. Drive to some local chain store and select one of their trees, plop it in the back of a pickup or trailer or car trunk, and take it home and plant it yourself (again) without reading the entirety of this book on how to do it correctly.

Now, I realize that many who are reading this book like to take short cuts, or you like a *deal*, or perhaps you can't afford to purchase a tree and have it planted by a professional, but you have to decide which category you're in and then act.

The absolute best way to select a tree and follow up on its growth, is to go to a nursery in your immediate area, select a tree that you can afford, and have them plant it for you! This way, your tree is **guaranteed** to have the best chance of growing healthily!

It depends on you to make tree selection and planting the easiest or the most difficult part of the entire process because it involves several people and we know that it isn't easy to please everyone.

To narrow down the decision, determine which trees are best for the area in which you live in the city. A tree, to grow fast and healthily, depends not only on the climate but also the soil conditions. As we move across Harris County and outlying areas, the climate is just about the same but the soil conditions vary from clay, to sandy loam, to sand, and combinations of each. This is why a local **nursery** can tell you **exactly** the best trees to choose for your area! Be smart, *please,* and follow what I'm telling you in this book. My *bio* says that I know about trees—and I do; my life has been with trees, and trees in this area! I'm not only your tree doctor but also the ER. Call me!

And like many doctors in other lines of work, if it doesn't work exactly as I say, please don't sue me. I can hardly **guarantee** the health or rate of growth of your tree, but I can guarantee that what I'm telling you give you the best *chance* of that tree(s) healthy survival.

Selecting a Tree

✔Make any type of rough sketch of your yard and how many trees you'd like to plant.

✔What do you **want** from a tree? Do you want shade? Do you want color? Do you want it to stay green all year long? Do you want one that grows fast? One that stays alive as long as you are alive?

✔ **Where** do you want this particular tree(s) to grow? In the front yard? Side yard? Back yard? Near the house for shade and to cut down on your a/c bill? Lot's of branches to be able to build a tree house for the kids when they grow a little? Maybe to block out the view of the neighbor's horrible new paint job? These questions, as silly as they sound, are what most people look for in a tree. There are maybe just a few trees that do what you want them to do, so the selection won't be difficult.

✔Now that you have this information, call the family together to sit down and select the tree(s) that you agree upon and you'll now be able to select wisely and quickly because you are armed with the proper information.

✔When the decision is made, all of you go to your closest *full-service nursery* with your rough sketch and ask for the manager who will either help or direct you to the person who can help.

The Best Place to Plant

There might have to be some changes in the type of tree or location at this point because it's not only the *area* in which you live, but also the soil conditions *in your particular yard;* irrigation, drainage, and nearness of the tree you selected to your walkway or house must also be considered.

I strongly suggest that if you have one or several trees to plant, that you go to a full-service nursery with a good reputation who has been in business—in Houston—long enough to know all about the trees in the area. They will know what works and what doesn't.

So, you have your sketch, the trees you'd like to have (or the one(s) your nursery advises), your family is in accordance with everything, and you are at your nursery. Now . . .

✔**Look** at the particular trees and determine the size, cost of buying them and the cost of having them planted for you. This way, you have a **full guarantee!**

The above steps are the best way to go if you can afford it. But since cost might be a determining factor, let's see what you can do to get the price down to where you can afford it. You see, I'm not for the nursery or for you—I'm for the trees! I want you to be happy with your trees and I'd like you to plant as many trees as you can afford.

Price

If, after you've priced the trees and the cost to have the nursery *plant* them is more than you can afford, you might buy the trees and plant them yourself. Be patient. I'll tell you how.

My next recommendation is to still follow the steps above and then, if you must, go to that neighborhood store (rather than not planting at all) with the information you've gotten from my book and from the nurseryman, and see which trees they have.

Few gardening stores, other than nurseries, have anyone around who knows much about trees even though they sell them. If you have read this book, you probably know more, or at least you know the right questions to ask.

Hopefully, you find the tree you want, and if so, have *them* place it for you in whatever means of transportation you have. If there are leaves on the tree, make certain these leaves are *covered with plastic* and securely fastened so you won't "burn" the leaves off with wind by the time you reach home.

Most of these large stores with a small section for plants and flowers, will have trees in different size pots. Rarely, in my experience, have they had the optimum size tree for planting; those in a 100-gallon container that are maybe 12 to 14 feet high with a trunk diameter of 3 to 4 inches.

If they don't have this size (or if the price is still too high) go for the 50-gallon, the 25 or lastly, the 5-gallon tree. I'd rather have you plant a seedling or a twig than not plant at all!

Actually, the **planting** of the tree is so *very important* that if your budget is such that you have to buy trees at a place other than a nursery, I'd still like you to have a professional *plant* the tree. If this is still more than you can pay, do read this next section on planting and transplanting.

I get more than 50 calls each week from people who want to know about the best tree to plant in their yard. I give them much of the information I'm giving you and I can do it without being suspect of guiding you to an expensive tree; **I don't sell trees!** I *treat* trees and *trim* trees, but I don't sell them. Now, let's look at the proper method to plant your tree.

Planting a Tree

The stories I hear from callers who have had difficulty before and after planting their own trees forces me to go into great detail when I tell you how to plant or transplant your trees.

You've selected your tree(s) and have it home safely, making certain it was wrapped to prevent leaf damage. Now, let's look at the *container* your tree is in. If it's in a burlap sack from a nursery, they will load it carefully for you and see that it is secure so it won't roll or shake thereby loosening the soil and damaging the roots.

When you take if off your vehicle, get help and be careful not to break up the root ball when transporting it to the planting site. The safest way to carry such a tree, if it's relatively small, is to cup your hands under the ball. If it's too large for you to handle alone, get help from a friend and slide it onto a tarp or wide board and carry it, together, gingerly, to the plant site and prepare to plant it.

Do not, under any conditions, grab the tree by the trunk or branches when you carry it!

If it's not to be planted for a day or so, make certain you keep it in a *shaded area* and cover the root ball with sawdust or peat moss and keep it *watered* so the root system won't dry out.

In planting the tree with burlap wrapping, there's no need to take the bag entirely off, just position it in the hole and peel it back or unfold as much of it as you can, thus keeping as much of the original dirt around the root system intact. Make certain the hole is at least **twice** as wide as the root ball and the exact depth as per this diagram.

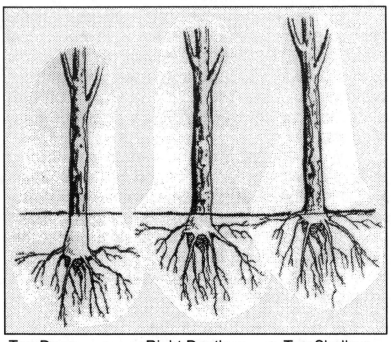

Too Deep   Right Depth   Too Shallow

This diagram is to show the depth of the roots to be planted whether it is burlap wrapped, one that you've taken from a container, or a bare root tree that you are planting or transplanting.

Many container trees (burlap wrapped, metal, plastic, or even wire wrapped) were probably planted in their container with special soil that is not like the soil in your yard. If you just dig a proper sized hole and lower the tree in, it may never root outside the nursery-mixed soil. Thus, you must **prepare the hole** to give your tree the best chance at survival.

Dig the hole *twice* as wide (as just about every plant book tells you) but remember, we are talking about the Houston area, which has more clay than most places. So, if you dig that hole but twice the size and it's in heavy clay, most of the time the root system will grow to this clay and turn around thus encircling the root ball causing the roots to bind the way you'll see plants do that are in an undersized pot.

What I'd like you to do to help that root system along, is dig 4 holes with a sharpshooter, at least as wide as that shovel and about as deep, and place them North, South, East and West, (diagram) thus creating a **passageway** for the roots to reach out to grow and thereby prevent them from circling the tree. It also helps secure this root system.

If the clay is really heavy, dig the hole twice as wide—and deep—and add *Soil Pro* or *Super Dirt*, soil

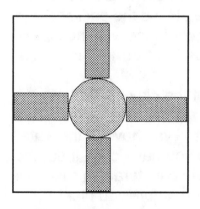

amendments that break up the clay soil. This works during excessively wet or dry situations by helping keep the water away from roots when it's too wet, and release the water when it's too dry. I'd add at least ¼ of the soil amendment to your soil and mix it all together.

Work a portion of all of this back into the hole until the root ball is at least an inch above the soil line and the rest around the roots. Then, top the area with mulch a few inches but keep the mulch off the bark of the tree. Now, water the area very well.

Do not add any fertilizer or root stimulator to the tree; the soil amendment and existing soil are sufficient; as long as you give the root system room to move and grow and keep it well watered, your tree has the best chance possible of being strong and healthy.

In addition to that, water the tree near the ends of each of these "trenches" thereby prompting the roots to go even farther out and search for water. In adding the soil, add the same soil as you dug up but make certain to break it up and turn it.

To further insure success, before you place your tree in the hole, get a product called **MycorTree** that contains spores of a beneficial fungus that helps to genetically alter the root systems where the tree can pick up food and water better. Read the package and apply as the label says in accordance with the size of your particular tree. It helps the tree in this hostile environment.

If you're not certain of the clay content of your soil, run a hose in the hole and fill it with water. This can also tell you the type of soil you have. If the water stays in the hole overnight, you have clay. If so, the spot is bad and the only way to counteract this is to till a 12'x12' area about 12" deep *before* you plant.

If the water drains, but slowly, go back to putting the four trenches around the original hole. This gives your tree an excellent chance of survival. Now, make certain it stays watered and fed.

On most of your smaller trees, the roots will be either wrapped in burlap, or in a container that is metal or plastic; here's how you do these. Get some sharp shears and begin at the top and cut down on opposite sides of the container, then fold these cut panels down disturbing the root system as little as possible.

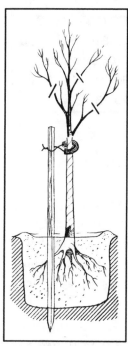

Staked tree

If the tree you selected needs support, put a long stake (wood, metal pipe, PVC plastic pipe, that is substantial) in the hole as you plant, and drive it in next to (not through) the root system for added support. Then tie your tree trunk to that stake as far up and down as you can to guide that tree to grow straight.

For ties, use plastic wrapped wires, cut off pieces of garden hose to prevent the wire from cutting into the trunk, or sturdy rope. Now, after 6 or 8 months, when the tree seems able to support itself, loosen these ties and give another month for the tree to adjust. If it does, remove the wire and stake entirely. If it hasn't adjusted by this time, call a tree expert or landscaper to see why that tree hasn' t rooted.

I see far too many trees where someone has staked them with a wire fastener (even with a hose over the wire) and forgotten to take it loose and the wire is cutting into the tree and choking it.

For a large tree that is planted or transplanted, your landscaper or tree service will know how to stake it. They will anchor it with guy wires that are fastened to pins that are attached to buried pipes or stakes and use compression rings to allow the tree to move naturally, but prevent high wind damage.

Transplanting a Tree

Let's suppose you got a deal from a friend who will give you a tree that is in their yard or on their farm. My experience is to accept (even **free)** trees that are maybe 10 feet tall or less that have a trunk diameter of 2 to 3 inches. You can handle these trees relatively easily alone or with the help of a friend.

The major effort in this undertaking is in **digging up** the tree; you have to make certain you get far enough around the root system so as not to throw the tree into absolute shock or kill it!

If you plan to burlap it or carry it in a container, get as much of the soil from where you dug up that tree and pack it around the roots. If this tree (or even one that you buy) is in a container for any length of time—like a few months or more—the roots might have circled at the bottom or sides and if this happens, when you dig your hole to plant it again, you might have to dig the hole wider than normal to handle these roots. Then, pull the roots out carefully with your hand

and spread them along the bottom of the hole before you start filling it up. Then, follow the planting procedure(s) I talked about above

You see, if you only dig the hole deeper and add mulch, within a matter of weeks that mulch (acting like a wet sponge) will flatten and the tree sinks farther than need be.

Root Barriers

A **Root Barrier** forms a **barricade** between the tree (and its roots) and the slab of your house that protects the slab from moisture-absorbing roots. Root growth varies with tree species, soil conditions, surface covering, rainfall, and irrigation practices. Root growth and function are essential for a healthy, sturdy tree, but roots can also cause problems. Roots crack and plug sewer lines; lift and break curbs, sidewalks, pavement, and building foundations.

In Houston, with such a preponderance of clay soil, this clay responds dramatically to moisture variations. During extended periods of rain, the soil gets wet and expands. When it's dry, usually from tree roots sucking out the water, it contracts, the slab settles, and structural damage occurs.

A mature Live Oak, for example, requires several **hundred** gallons of water each day. If this tree's root system is left unrestricted, it searches for water wherever it can find it, and the best source is under your house. Large amounts of water are then sucked in *from* under the house, the soil dries, and what's left is a lot of air. When this air compresses (you can squeeze 55 gallons of air into a thimble) the slab settles, tilts and cracks.

Generally, the problems are gradual. The first sign might be that a door sticks. Then, hairline cracks appear in the sheetrock or plaster above the doors or windows. This could lead to a major problem like the severely cracked slab in my story on page 17 with that man and his $40,000 repair job. If you notice a problem, your first step should be to call a **structural** engineer who specializes in slabs.

To better explain how this occurs, this next page shows a drawing that my wife, Lisa, did of a tree and its root system. Most people hear that if you turn a tree upside down, that the root system is the same size— **wrong!** The roots extend **twice**, sometimes **three** times the radius of the canopy with only the tap roots burrowing deep.

Now, to *prevent* these tree roots from drinking from under your house, enter the **ROOT BARRIER.** Foster's process is to install a stiff non-biodegradable shield that is buried between the tree and your slab. The root barrier that my company uses was either invented by, or improved upon by my father.

We're not the only company that installs root barriers; if installed by a reputable, knowledgeable company, this root barricade (barrier) gives you both the advantage of saving your foundation and allows you to keep your tree(s).

*Tree roots, unlike what is commonly believed, are not as large as the tree itself. The feeder roots grow (usually) no deeper than 12 " and spread out to, even **three** times the width of the tree.*

A root barrier is made of ¼" thick, high density *Polyethylene*, which is the same strength as a ½" thick *Plexiglass* (the stuff used for bulletproof glass) to form a 2 foot-high barrier.

Then, a trench (usually 30" deep to be certain) is dug—by hand—2 to 3 feet from the foundation of the home and the cut and welded Polyethylene is lowered into the open trench so that it becomes one continuous barricade.

This is not a process that is easily done by the homeowner. And, some companies that install Root Barriers aren't using the proper materials or taking the extra precautions we do to protect the foundation or the trees.

The very **worst** I've seen happen is when a **trenching machine** is used, it literally **grabs, tears** and **pulls** tree roots as it digs the trench to install a barricade. This destroys feeder and hair roots that are important to the survival of the tree; it rips these roots so far back that the tree's chance of survival is nil. You might not know it for a year or so, but your tree will die! As a homeowner, watch out for this and ask questions.

> The best method is the "old fashioned" way; **hand dig** the trench for the sake of the tree and to avoid busting up underground utilities.

Willow, Poplar, and Maple are some landscape trees that have invasive roots and will *seek out* a sewer line, septic tank or drain. Only small trees should be planted in such areas. Again, you truly **should have** a professional help select your trees.

Many cities are using devices to wrap sewer pipes but these aren't flawless. Some cities install special watertight flexible telescopic joints for sewer lines in new building sites to *minimize* these problems, but they still arise. Some contractors wrap sewer joints with a copper wire screen (toxic to small roots) but when large roots crack the pipe, the small roots enter and clog the drain.

Some contractors wrap sewer lines with a root-resistant geotextile which does, in fact, *keep out* invading roots but again, it will not prevent joint or pipe cracking by the larger roots and when there's a crack, the smaller roots are there thirsting for a drink. And, the **wrong** tree in a small planting site will, without a doubt, cause costly damage.

Cracked Slabs

I don't mean to be butting in on **Tom Tynan's** area of expertise in talking about foundations, but since trees cause most of the foundation damage, please follow what I'm about to tell you. It could save you **thousands** of dollars when you try to sell your house.

In purchasing a home that has evidence of the slab cracking, or if you live in a home and begin to notice this door-sticking, sheetrock-lines-showing problem, hire an **independent structural engineer** to inspect your home before calling anyone else. They will tell you whether to call a foundation company, an irrigation company, or a tree company.

The engineering company will conduct an inspection and give you an *unbiased* finding, along with their recommendations, that gives you but one blueprint to follow. Then, I suggest you call several companies to bid this work. This way, one company cannot use inferior materials or shoddy workmanship to cut the cost; you will be comparing "apples to apples."

It is also important to keep **documentation** in a safe place for the future sale of your home. Here are a few examples:

*One homeowner had foundation problems caused by tree roots and the slab had tilted 2 to 3 inches. We got the call, determined what the problem was, and installed a root barricade (barrier). Three years later the homeowner put his home up for sale. The finance company sent in an engineer who reported a **one inch drop** in the slab. The deal was turned down!*

*Same problem as with the homeowner above. Except, **this** homeowner called in a **structural engineer**. After inspecting the slab (it had fallen 2 or 3 inches) the engineer sent the man a 6-page report describing in detail, the present condition of the slab and suggested the man call us. We did root barricading (same as above).*

*A few years later when he put his house on the market, the finance company sent out **their** engineer (same as above) and the finance company again planned to turn the financing of the house down. But, the homeowner produced his **engineer's report** from a few years back and because of the root barrier, the slab improved a few inches. The loan was then approved and the man sold his house.*

You see, the finance company relies on their engineer to make a finding, and an engineer won't take the word of a tree company. But, they will take evidence from a written report by another engineer.

Trees I Suggest You Plant

Now we're down to the trees that grow best in Houston and the surrounding areas, and those that "might" grow healthy and strong. There are many more varieties of oaks than I plan to mention here and that's because I will tell you what you need to know about the *best trees* with some information about the ones you might have that are not good "marriages" for our soil and weather conditions.

Before I begin on the types of trees, I'm going to (forgive the pun) "go out on a limb" to share with you what my understanding is for fast, slow or medium-growth in trees—**usually!** Fast growth is when a tree reaches maturity in 2½ to 3 years; medium growth could be 5 to 10, and slow growth, 15 years on. I have read book after book and I can't recall finding one that has a growth chart anywhere. I guess authors of tree books, assuming they are arborists, know that the growth depends on so many factors.

Trees grow fast or slow in different parts of the world because of the **climate** and **soil conditions**. Growth also depends on how they are watered and fertilized. And then there are two trees planted within 50 feet of each other—the same everything—yet one grows faster and taller and thicker than the other. My fast, medium and slow tree growth is an approximation from my own experiences.

In Houston you'll find the Live Oak, the Water Oak, the Post Oak, Nutall Oak, Shumard Red Oak and some Willow Oaks, probably more Live Oaks than any other. My first choice is the LIVE OAK.

LIVE OAK—grows as high as 50 feet with a heavy limb spread of about 75 feet. It likes full sun and will grow in just about any soil but grows best in well-drained clay and gravelly clay loam. It does not tolerate poorly drained soils or extremely well-drained deep sands and does best on neutral to only slightly acidic soils.

Temperature can be critical for this majestic tree. Live Oaks were almost completely destroyed in Dallas during the winter of 1983 when the temperature was below freezing for more than 12 days. In the Houston area, I can't recall when it was that cold for that long a period of time.

Live Oak

The Live Oak lives longer than any of the other trees but can take 15 or more years to reach its maximum height. It has a strong bark, its limbs are as "break resistant" as any trees around, it fends off most insects and diseases (except Oak Wilt) and if you plant one as a boy it will probably outlive your great grandchildren.

Yet another nice feature of the Live Oak is that it is semi-evergreen, in that it has a slow dormancy from March through May putting on new leaves just about as fast as it drops old leaves, making the appearance of the tree never losing its leaves.

The few minuses it has are that it needs a large

The few minuses it has are that it needs a large space for its extensive root system and it takes huge amounts of water. It's great for large back yards.

SHUMARD RED OAK —likes sun, moist soil and good drainage. A great tree for the Houston area because it's durable, has a medium growth rate and reaches maturity faster than a Live Oak or Water Oak. It is more tolerant of alkaline soil and grows well in a city environment. The summer foliage is green and the fall foliage stands out in an array or reddish bronze leaves. It's normal "city" height is about 60' and as wide as 40' with exceptions

Shumard Red Oak

that reach 120' in the rich, moist bottom land soils in the Pineywoods and Gulf Prairies. It lives from 40 to 60 years and has a good shape, with a uniform limb structure.

It is prone to *fungus* and *chlorosis* (plant version of *anemia*—lack of iron) and must be kept watered and fed.

DRUMMOND RED MAPLE—is a beautiful tree because of the bright crimson and scarlets it exhibits in any season. During winter the fat red buds brighten the dark, upper reaches of the bare forest canopy. In February, long before the leaves unfold, the stamens of the male flowers are rosy pink to bright red. The trees then produce flaming orbs of drooping clusters of bright pink and brilliant red samaras (a one-seeded fruit).

Drummond Red Maple

These gorgeous trees are the showiest in the fall, when the leaves turn to shades of crimson and scarlet. It is deciduous (leaves fall off) in the winter months and if any leaves remain, they turn to a red or yellow tint.

It is a fast growing tree and gets to about 65 feet high with a canopy span of 35 feet but has been known to grow to 90 feet tall.

BRADFORD PEAR—a truly lovely tree for any front yard! It grows rather quickly to a height of about 25 feet with a canopy of 15 feet. It grows upright with little help and begins in a sort of pyramidal shape then later in an oval shape. It likes full sun, very good drainage and fertile soil. It is less

Bradford Pear

susceptible to fire-blight disease than other pear trees.

In fall, the leaves are purple to copper-colored that change to a profusion of white flowers in early spring. (The *Aristocrat* is a smaller, wider, nearly oval tree.) When buying one, be certain to inquire if it is a blooming *cultivar* (family members) like the Flowering or Ornamental Pear trees that might be stronger and more disease resistant.

GREEN ASH & WHITE ASH—two excellent trees for this area. The Green Ash likes sun and some shade and grows best in moist, organic soils. It likes water and can get to 80 feet with a canopy of about 40 feet. It also grows well on heavy limestone clays and acid sands and sandy loams. But liking moisture, does best along rivers, streams, ponds, flood plains and in swales and depressions.

Green Ash

It is a medium to fast growth tree (which I like) and gets tall enough to make an impression in 5 to 7 years. It is an excellent shade tree and in fall, the leaves are yellow to purple. Most White Ash and Green Ash trees live to 50, 60, 75 years and longer.

WHITE ASH differs only slightly from the Green Ash in that it prefers well-drained soil, and grows as tall as 100 feet though most are about 75 feet at maturity.

The male and female flowers are produced on separate trees in April and May. The male trees flower yearly, but the female trees flower and fruit only every 3 to 5 years. The leaves are deciduous and turn to delicate pastel shades of pink, orange, and purple in autumn. They are *pinnately* (leaves on each side of a stem resembling a feather) compound with five to nine leaflets; seven is the usual number. Its leaves are more oval and have a yellow fall coloring. It too lives 60, 70 or so years and needs much water to grow its tallest and to extend its life span. Several are reported to live more than 100 years.

High Maintenance Trees

Below are some trees that grow in Houston that I have to attend to more than the above. I'm not saying that I don't like them or that they are undesirable trees, with the exception of the ARIZONA ASH, a tree that is extremely troublesome.

ARIZONA ASH—grows to maybe 50 feet and has a canopy almost as wide, likes sun, moist fertile soil, but will grow okay with some shade and has a low water requirement. Although it grows to maturity in 3 to 5 years, it often lives only 5 to

Arizona Ash

12 years (sometimes 15 to 30 in this climate) and is brittle and highly prone to damage from disease and insects.

Because of its rapid growth rate, it is easily raised from seed and reasonably inexpensive, many builders who probably don't know better, have planted them all over the Houston area. My suggestion is if you have one that is dying, take it down and plant one of the trees I recommend.

WILLOW OAK—Grows great in full sun but likes moist soil conditions with good drainage. It gets to a height of about 75 feet with a spread of maybe 45 feet. They resist insects as does the Live Oak but it isn't as disease resistant as the Live Oak and is subject to *leaf spot, fungus* and *chlorosis*. Lives about 60-80 years and is an excellent shade tree. You'll be able to recognize it from the rest because of it's elongated leaves that resemble a willow leaf.

This tree grows best in the wetter soils of eastern Texas and many are in water several feet high, but usually in areas that flood 6-8 months each year. You'll see them in Houston but they are high in maintenance. A shame, because it is a truly different looking, attractive and provocative tree. Its best areas are the Piney Woods, Gulf Prairies and Marshes from Brazoria County to the east, as well as the stream bottoms and flooded drainage ways of the Post Oak Savannah.

I have a personal dislike for Willow Oaks even though they are gorgeous trees, because they are **quitters;** if they get a disease or a fungus, they give up. If you already have one, take care of it. But my advice is not to buy one; go for the Live Oak!

WATER OAK—grows fast to a height of almost 50 feet with a width of 35 feet. There are many Water Oaks that grow to heights of almost 80 feet but its love of water makes it grow best in swamps, low flats, and stream banks in the Post Oak Savannah, Pineywoods, and Gulf Prairies and Marshes.

It is a part of a family consisting of Willow, Water, and Laurel Oaks and their hybrids, all of which are not easy to identify. It likes sun, a clay-based soil, and lots of moisture. If found in Houston, they grow best along canals, ditches or bayous. If it's grown in alkaline soil, it will develop *iron chlorosis* and draws insects and is more prone to *Anthracnose*, but it can withstand poor drainage. It grows fast and reaches maturity in 6 to 8 years. It has dark green, spoon-shaped leaves that vary in persistence from completely deciduous to almost completely evergreen.

SILVER LEAF MAPLE—is a tree that I am in a dilemma over. Many people in this area already have these trees so I'll tell you why I have problems in actually recommending that you plant them.

It's a beautiful tree, silvery on the underside of its leaves, and grows to about 80 feet with a spread of 40 feet. It requires excellent drainage, and can take ordinary soil and sun.

But, it has *weak wood* making it more prone to disease, insects, sun scald and cankers. It has shallow roots that interfere with nearby plants and its vigorous root system invades drain lines, breaks and buckles pavement, and it's also messy. It grows fast but is short lived, 15 to 25 years. The *Drummond Red Maple* is more preferable in this part of the country.

BALD CYPRESS—will grow in relatively well-drained areas, but does better in the wetter areas. An average height is 45 feet with a canopy of 20 feet in a conical form that resembles a large Christmas tree. It has a medium growth rate and lives long 50 to 60 years, sometimes longer. It is prone to attract *European Red Spider Mites* and its "knees" might protrude in your yard.

Cypress

It has a feathery bright green foliage in spring and a coppery red/brown leaf coloring in fall. The knees arise from the roots in extremely wet areas (swamps, near a lake, in a lake) that measure from a few inches to more than 6 feet tall. If growing in water, these knees roam far above the surface and become hollow with age.

The Bald Cypress tree is native of East Texas swamps and older ones reach a height of 130 feet with a 70-foot spread. There is also a *Montezuma Bald Cypress* that grows less than 50 feet tall but has difficulty surviving even the moderate winters in Houston and can become deciduous.

In the gardens of *Chapultepec* grows the **Cypress of Montezuma**, which in 1900 measured more than 168 feet tall and 50 feet in circumference. And, **El Giante**, that grows in the churchyard at *Santa Maria del Tule* in *Oaxaca, Mexico,* that stands 140 feet tall and measures 150 feet in circumference. This tree is believed to be from 1,500 to 2,000 years old.

PECAN TREE—a tree that is *everywhere* and I, reluctantly, have to talk down about pecan trees although it seems that everyone wants a pecan tree. They are among my least favorite (from the homeowner's pocketbook) tree in the area because they are truly difficult to keep healthy.

Pecan Tree

■They need constant care and maintenance for them to grow pecans.

■They are subject to a myriad of diseases and pests.

■The limbs are brittle and often break.

■They attract squirrels which eat the pecans, and leave the shells all over the ground. If you'll notice in most pecan trees there are dead limbs and brown leaves just *hanging* there from squirrels that chew on the small limbs, causing them to die.

■Although the pecan tree is the **State Tree of Texas**,

it truly *is* messy on a home lot. Not only does it drop leaves and limbs periodically, it is subject to damage from a long list of diseases. The nuts from a pecan tree quickly grow wherever they drop, or wherever a squirrel plants them, and puts down a deep root so rapidly that even a seedling but one foot high is difficult to pull from a flower bed.

The production of pecans is dependent on the species of pecan tree, the water, and the health of that tree. A schedule for spraying can be obtained from your *County Extension Agent* or perhaps your nursery. This spray schedule, however, is not cost-effective for small crops. Most people use *Malathion,* perhaps because it smells so strong they feel it is good. On the contrary, Malathion is used on food crops and is so UN-potent that you can eat the fruit in a few days. On plants, vegetables (and pecan trees) the spray is effective for as long as three weeks.

Pecan trees abound in this area; some grow to a height of 100 feet tall with a spread of from 65 to 75 feet. Smaller sizes have been developed, the dwarf. Get info on these from your nurseryman. If you want pecans to eat, it is better to go to a shop that sells pecans.

If you get an insect or a disease on a tomato plant, for instance, you simply get some *Malathion* or *Sevin* and spray the plant. Well, same treatment for a pecan tree but a bit more difficult trying to get **80 feet up in the air** with a span that is maybe 65 feet wide. It's troublesome and dangerous to spray and maintain yourself and expensive when you have some tree company do it for you.

> If one tree is infected by a fungus or bacteria in your yard, all the other trees must be treated. Professionals will never treat a single tree unless it is isolated.

MAGNOLIAS—have several species. The one I would recommend that you **never** grow in a yard (unless you have a large farm) is the *Southern Magnolia*; it grows to 60 feet with a width of about 35 feet. Its root system, however, spreads and spreads and grows near the surface so never add fill dirt or flower beds, it could kill the tree! It likes a loose, acid, fertile soil with lots of organic matter.

Magnolia

It's best never to prune a Magnolia. It automatically prunes itself, thus building a leaf mulch underneath the canopy similar to forest trees. This enables them to feed themselves. They shed leaves all year.

Now, there is a delightful Magnolia called the *Star,* that is gorgeous for front yards. It grows to only about 9 feet with a 6-foot canopy and displays fragrant white flowers in January. This *Star Magnolia* likes full sun or part shade and well-drained, fertile soil and needs water only when it is dry.

The CHINESE TALLOW is called a *trash tree* by most nurserymen, but do you know what? **I like the tree**. It grows quickly (35 feet high with a spread of about 30 feet), needs little or no maintenance, tolerates sun or shade, grows in just about everything short of cement, and if you cut it down in January, its back up in May. You can cut and trim the branches unmercifully and it doesn't seem to affect the health or life of the tree.

Chinese Tallow

It has a nice blend of yellow, red, orange and purple in fall and is a bright green in summer. It has small leaves, with little white berries (or green) on it that give it character. You'll see Chinese Tallow trees growing in vacant lots and on suburban acreage by the thousands. They need little maintenance, and live to about 15 or 20 years old then, eventually, have to be cut down.

These are popular trees on many area golf courses, especially ones that need trees because Chinese Tallow do seem to grow overnight and although not a great tree, it has its moments.

PINE TREES—are my *least favorite* of all time, in a homeowners yard, in spite of their majestic beauty. I feel the minuses far outweigh the beauty. For instance, they emit a glue-like substance on the needles that if it gets on your roof and is allowed to remain, is strong enough to eat through most of your shingles. Or clumps of these needles adhere easily to most composition roofs, and if allowed to gather water and remain very long, they will cause roof rot. The pine cones are fine at Christmas for making wreaths or decorations but to a lawn mower blade it's the same as cutting stones.

The one you'll see most is the *LOBLOLLY PINE* that grows as high as 80 feet with needled-strewn branches that extend out over a 35-foot canopy. Shortleaf and Longleaf Pine run rampant in East Texas.

Pine trees grow quickly; 3½" height and ½" trunk diameter per year when young, and to over 60 feet tall in 20 years. Furthermore, it is very susceptible to Fusiform Gall Rust, and the Pine Bark Beetle.

Risk Management—Insurance

There is an assumption that insurance makes things more expensive, but how expensive is a valuable asset that you can't afford to replace? Quality does, in fact, cost a little more.

When seeking a quality contractor, *always* verify their insurance coverage. *Before* you allow anyone to work in your yard or on your house, ask them to mail or fax a copy of their certificate of insurance to you. Then place a telephone call to their **insurance company** and ask if these policies are **still** in effect.

First, **General Liability** covers damage to people and to things on your property; accidents **do** happen! If a tree damages your house (or your neighbor's house, fence or garage) and the contractor drives away, *you pay!*

Also, check for **Workers Compensation** (*not mandatory* in **Texas).** If a worker gets hurt while working on your property, they could sue *you* for hospital bills and personal injury.

If you get a "deal" from someone who has no insurance, I know it's tempting to save a few hundred dollars, but the risk far exceeds the savings!

©County Extension Agents in Your Area:

❖Houston and Harris County (713) 221-5020
❖Brazoria County 713-849-5711
❖Galveston County 713-534-3413
❖Montgomery County 409-539-7824

Tree Removal Companies

Eric Grayson, the tree expert who works for me, says, "You can pay $400 or $4,000 to remove a tree, but the tree is just as removed at either price!"

You don't need to call the *best* tree company in town to **take out** a tree; just be certain they have **good insurance coverage**! You can't hurt the tree when you remove it. Call several companies to get the lowest bid. I usually direct people to tree removal companies that clear lines for the light company; they are insured and reasonably priced.

❖Davey Trees, (713) 973-8733 (line clearers)

❖Trees, Inc., (713) 692-6371 (line clearers)
❖Don's Tree Company, (713) 774-3330 (competitive)
❖Westheimer Trees, (713) 782-5241 (especially with
   trees near the street; they have a boom truck)

Tree Pruning Companies

Selective pruning is done every 5 to 6 years. Someone *other* than a specialist can come out every year or two and remove broken or low hanging limbs, sucker growth, or to shape your trees. Below are some companies that I highly recommend.

❖Timber Green, (713) 695-7695 Ask for Bob Davis.
❖Trees Unlimited, (713) 688-6739, Jim Blanchard
❖Greentree Experts, 1-800-895-7212
❖Don's Tree Service, (713) 774-3330 Meyerland area

Full-Service Nurseries

❖Hampton Gardens Landscaping, 1832 Bissonnet,
   (713) 528-4984, Barbara Day
❖Bill Bownds Nursery, 2815 Campbell Road,
   (713) 462-6447, and 10519 FM 1464 Sugar Land,
   (281) 277-2033
❖RCW Nurseries, 15809 SH 249, (281) 440-5161
❖Wolfe's Nurseries, Houston, Humble & Katy
❖Tree Search Farms, 7625 Alabonson, (713) 937-9811
❖Cornelius Nurseries, Voss Road, (713) 782-8640;
   FM1960, (281) 444-1210; Dairy Ashford,
   (281) 493-0550

Stump Removal

❖Dean's Stump Removal, (281) 394-0417

Structural Engineers

❖Peverly Engineering, (713) 977-0328

Foundation Companies

❖Atlas Foundations, (713) 641-4844
❖AAA Foundations, (713) 467-8981

SPECIAL NOTE: From time to time I get a call from a homeowner whose tree was damaged or killed by a neighbor, a utility company or some other service company. The person to call in this instance is JACK **HILL**, a **Forensic Consultant**, who will evaluate the cost of the damage and present it in a court of law. His number in Conroe is **(409) 756-3041**; In Houston, **(713) 447-2111**.

ABOUT the AUTHOR

John Foster is a 4th generation "Tree Man." His grandfather and great-grandfather were Lumbermen; they knew their trees. Although they were in the business of *cutting trees* which is frowned upon today by environmentalists everywhere, there are still those around who cut trees in planned and managed areas, a profession known as "Urban Forestry."

John's father, Ove (O.V.) made a decision early in life to study the physiology of trees. He dedicated more than half his life to the preservation of valuable trees in the Texas Gulf Coast area. His name was known throughout the area as the "Arborist to call when a homeowner needed help with their trees."

John grew up around such notable characters as Bill Zak, John Burrow, Dewey Compton, and his dad. Dewey Compton, became famous for his vast knowledge about the health and growth conditions of plants and trees in all of Texas. Bill Zak and John Burrow won their fame as co-hosts of the KTRH GardenLine show which has aired for more than 46 years. Bill Zak retired at the beginning of 1996 and now John Burrow, who's been with the show for more than 10 years, has a new co-host, Randy Lemmon, a Texas A&M graduate.

While most of his friends were out playing baseball or football, John spent his afternoons with his dad, diagnosing tree problems. It soon became second nature for Ove to ask young John's opinion on various trees and, at age 14, John was one of the youngest persons in the state to become licensed by the Structural Pest Control Board, the state agency governing licensing of both certified applicators and the diagnosis of problems in trees.

In 1983 John went to California for over a year to work for the Forestry Department, learning more about the physiology of trees. Thus, his hands-on experience and general knowledge has made him one of the foremost authorities on trees for the Texas Gulf Coast.

John's love for trees in evident in his expression as he leans against a tree or surveys it for damage, and he gives straight answers to homeowners. He tells them approximately how long their tree will live, that he can keep it alive for so many months or years, or when he feels they will have to cut it down. Whatever the answer, you can be certain that it's the truth and that it's told to you by an expert.

About the Author information written by Linda Grayson.

About the Publisher
by John Foster

This is my first book. After a lifetime of talking to people about trees, I decided to try and put some of it down on paper. It sounded easy. I had sufficient information on trees in my head to fill a dozen books, but I quickly learned that there was a vast difference between what's in your head and what you can get down on paper. This is where my publisher, Pete Billac, comes in.

He became my coach, my editor, critic and conscience. During the time we worked together, Pete seemed to eat, drink, and sleep tree problems. He spent several days with me on my daily consultations and asked many, many questions providing a sort of sounding board to help me organize my thoughts. By the time we finished the book, he knew more about trees than most of the people in the business.

If you ever decide to put your story or your life's work into a book, you can trust Pete Billac and SWAN Publishing; they know how to do it. And if you do, be prepared to work! When Pete is "on the case" he gets very serious. To keep his pace, you will need to be on all eight cylinders. He is also fun to work with. He'll make you laugh with him, at him, and laugh at yourself.

One of his favorite sayings is, "A monkey can **write** a book, but it takes a hard working, smart, **team** of monkeys to market it." From this, I got the feeling that he was setting me up to market the book when it's completed. His next comment made me know that what

I suspected was true. "Most writers," he said, "think they can write a book then sail away on their yacht to Tahiti with the royalties. It rarely to never happens that way."

Pete edited and published four books on KTRH Homeowner Hotline host Tom Tynan, and two for KTRH GardenLine host, John Burrow. He has one on Dr. David Mobley of KSEV, and wrote one titled THE LAST MEDAL OF HONOR about Vietnam war hero, MSG. Roy Benavidez of nearby El Campo. Pete's most recent books are ALL ABOUT CRUISES and NEW FATHER'S BABY GUIDE. Two other books, HOW NOT TO BE LONELY (for women) and then, HOW NOT TO BE LONELY **TONIGHT** (for men) sold over 3 million copies!

Pete, you told me I needed one more page to make the book come out even. I hope you print this because I do thank you for your, guidance, patience and professionalism.

Other Books by Swan Publishing

HOW NOT TO BE LONELY . . . If you're about to marry, recently divorced or widowed, want to forgive, forget or both, this is an excellent book; candid, positive, entertaining and informative —a fun book to read with answers that will help you get a date or a mate. It tells you where to find them, what to say and how to keep them. (Over 3 million copies sold) . . . . $ 9.95

HOW NOT TO BE LONELY *TONIGHT* . . . The sequel for the *MALE* reader. Other than being courageous and strong, smart women want their man to be sensitive, caring, and understanding. "The" book to give to your man. Or, for men who really want to learn what turns the modern woman on . . . . $ 9.95

NEW FATHER'S BABY GUIDE . . . Another best selling book by Pete Billac. The **perfect gift** for ALL new fathers. There is not a book for new fathers quite like this one! Tells (dummy dad) about Lamaze classes, burping, feeding and changing the baby plus 40 side-splitting drawings by athlete/cartoonist Cash Lambin. Most of all, it tells dad how to **SPOIL** mom! **GET IT** for that new daddy! . . . . $ 9.95

HOW TO BUY A NEW CAR & SAVE THOU$ANDS . . . Inside information on dealerships and salespersons. This book by Cliff Evans, a former car salesman and general manager, really **will** save you thousands on your next new car purchase . $ 9.95

A WOMAN'S GUIDE TO SEXUAL ENHANCEMENT. . . or REVERSING IMPOTENCE *FOREVER* . . . A truly great book written by two world famous urologists, Dr. David F. Mobley and Dr. Steven K. Wilson. This books tells MEN how they can REVERSE this problem complete with many drawings which show how impotence can be reversed and is **perfect** for the woman to read, then "slip it" under her partner's pillow . $ 9.95

ALL ABOUT CRUISES—Shirley Ragusa (cruise expert) and Pete Billac (63 cruises) tells everything first-time cruisers need to know, about which cruise ships to take, the best deals, shopping, packing, tours, etc. **The best cruise book available!** . . . $ 9.95

BOOKS BY TOM TYNAN:

Volume 1. Home Improvement (Homeowner's most often asked questions) saves you thousands of dollars on easy-to repair-items in your home that **you** can do! . . . . $ 9.95

Volume 2. Building and Remodeling. Whether you should do it or have it done. How to choose a contractor, subs, get a loan, call an inspection, get permits, insurance, architects, etc. $ 9.95

Volume 3. Buying & Selling A Home. A book used by many Realtors. Secrets on selling and on buying . What to fix and, what **not** to fix. What to paint. What to clean. A **great** book! . $ 9.95

Volume 4. Step by Step (15 energy-saving projects) that will save you money on your energy bills . . . . $ 9.95

BOOKS BY JOHN BURROW:

Your Front Yard—everything you need to know about growing healthy grass, shrubs and flowers. A book with answers most homeowners are afraid to ask. A quick reference guide. . .$ 9.95

Vegetable Gardening (Spring & Fall) what to grow and when to grow it; in city, country, even patio gardens. Vegetables from A to Z. The vegetable book planting guide for Texas . . . $ 9.95

JOHN FOSTER is available for personal appearances, luncheons, banquets, seminars, etc. Call (281) 388-3547 for cost and availability.

For each book, send a personal check or money order in the amount of $12.85 per copy to:
Swan Publishing, 126 Live Oak, Alvin, TX, 77511.

LIBRARIES—BOOKSTORES—QUANTITY ORDERS

**Swan Publishing
126 Live Oak
Alvin, TX 77511**

To order by major credit card 24 hours a day call:
(281) 268-6776 or long distance 1-800-866-8962
Fax: (281) 585-3738

Delivery in 2-7 days